International Treasures

Canberra's Embassies

Dorothy Hart
Artist Isla Patterson

First published in 2017 by Barrallier Books Pty Ltd,
trading as Echo Books

Registered Office: 35-37 Gordon Avenue, West Geelong, Victoria 3220, Australia.

www.echobooks.com.au

Copyright © Dorothy Hart and Isla Patterson

National Library of Australia Cataloguing-in-Publication entry.

Author: Hart, Dorothy, author.

Title: International treasures : Canberra's embassies / Dorothy Hart ; Isla Patterson.

ISBN: 9780648202530 (paperback)

Subjects: Diplomatic and consular service--Australian Capital Territory--Canberra--History. Embassy buildings--Australian Capital Territory--Canberra--History.

Other Creators/Contributors: Patterson, Isla, illustrator.

Book and cover design by Peter Gamble, Canberra.
Set in Garamond Premier Pro Display, 12/17 and Aqualine Two.

Front cover illustration: *South African High Commission residence 'South Africa House'* (2002)

Back cover illustration: *Entrance detail, Brazillian Embassy residence* (2001)

Art Copyright © Isla Patterson

www.echobooks.com.au

Foreword

Most of us would only have a peripheral understanding of the critical and enduring role played by the diplomat in the conduct of a nation's affairs. Any knowledge we do acquire tends to come from brief television footage, newspaper or radio comment on the pronouncements of world leaders and their foreign ministers primarily in relation to important security, trade and immigration matters.

The formulation of these generally brief policy statements is invariably the product of long and sometimes intense diplomatic discourse between nations, conducted through the aegis of involved diplomatic missions.

Most heads of mission are professional diplomats, some are not; whatever the case, their primary function is the same, to represent their nation's interests to the government of the country to which they are formally accredited. To do this, Ambassadors and High Commissioners are supported by quality staffs with expertise in political, trade, defence and cultural matters along with other skills appropriate to the size and focus of the Mission.

Diplomacy, as an essential arm of communications between royal rulers of yesteryear and then between governments, was more formally established in 1815 through the aegis of the Congress of Vienna. Earlier iterations included the employment of monks in the Middle Ages and heralds, followed by the appointment, for the first time, of full time ambassadors by Italy in the 15th century.

In Australia, the United Kingdom established the first diplomatic mission in 1935, followed by the United States in 1939; the latter building its mission in Canberra in the style of a lovely southern mansion. This lead to other countries following suit in building beautiful missions incorporating architecture peculiar to those countries.

Dorothy Hart, to her great credit and for the cultural benefit of all Australians, has produced this timely, stimulating and superbly illustrated book on the architectural history of thirty-six of Canberra's High Commissions and Embassies. She has been magnificently supported by the well-known Canberra artist, Isla Patterson, whose watercolours of each Chancery add beauty, life and interest to Dorothy's written word.

What I also found fascinating in each story was a clear explanation—beautifully reproduced—of the history of each national flag. A comprehensive list of all foreign embassies and high commissions in Australia is a useful ready-reference.

I think it also appropriate to thank the participating missions for their enthusiastic support of the project. I trust that the resulting positive publicity will achieve an even closer linkage between Missions and the Australian community.

Dorothy Hart and Isla Patterson, in years of skilled and co-operative endeavour, have together displayed extraordinary commitment to a most worthy and informative cause: the beautifully written and painted architectural histories of the Chancery buildings of thirty-six nations accredited to Australia.

I commend *International Treasures. Canberra's Embassies* to the widest possible readership.

Major General the Hon Michael Jeffery, AC, AO(Mil), CVO, MC (Ret'd)
Canberra

Michael Jeffery

February 2017

Contents

Embassies and High Commissions presented

Introduction	1
Embassy of Belgium	4
Embassy of Bosnia/Herzegovina	6
Embassy of Botswana	8
Embassy of Brazil	10
High Commission of Canada	12
Embassy of China	14
Embassy of Croatia	16
Delegation of the European Union	18
High Commission of Fiji	20
Embassy of Finland and Estonia	22
Embassy of France	24
Embassy of Greece	26
Embassy of Hungary	28
High Commission of India	30
Embassy of Indonesia	32
Embassy of Ireland	34
Embassy of Italy	36
Embassy of Japan	38
High Commission of Malaysia	40

Contents

Embassy of Mexico	42
Embassy of Myanmar	44
Embassy of Netherlands	46
High Commission of New Zealand	48
High Commission of Papua New Guinea	50
Embassy of Philippines	52
Embassy of Poland	54
Embassy of Saudi Arabia	56
High Commission of Singapore	58
High Commission of South Africa	60
Embassy of Spain	62
Embassy of Sweden	64
Embassy of Switzerland	66
Embassy of Thailand	68
Embassy of Turkey	70
High Commission of United Kingdom	72
Embassy of United States of America	74
Addresses of all Embassies and High Commissions represented in Canberra	76

Acknowledgements

Our very special thanks to the diplomatic staff of the Embassies and High Commissions who have co-operated and encouraged us and supplied data for our book.

Thanks also to Echo Books, Ian Gordon and Peter Gamble for not only publishing our book but also for their patience and assistance at all times.

To Major General Michael Jeffery, AC, AO(Mil), CVO, MC (Retd) for writing a Foreword to our book.

To the ACT Writers Centre for their many writers workshops which have been extremely helpful.

To the Department of Foreign Affairs and Trade for their numerous publications.

Thanks to Rhonda Whitton, author and teacher, who gave great encouragement and advice in the early stages of our research.

To Len Olijnyk, AIPP (Australian Institute of Professional Photographers), RSASA (Royal South Australian Society of Arts) for his photography of Isla's paintings.

To Ann Oner for editing final book proof.

And special thanks to our husbands, Steve and Jeffrey, who have worked silently behind the scenes editing, collating and annotating pictures and text as well as help with IT.

About the Author

Dorothy Hart graduated with a B. Commerce (Melbourne University), a B. Arts-History major (Queensland University) and a Grad. Dip. in Local and Applied History (University of New England). She has been involved in economic and history research both in the government and corporate sectors. She was the voluntary Public Relations Officer for the Regular Defence Welfare Association for many years.

Passionate about history and heritage, she is a member of the Canberra and Yass Districts Historical Societies and the National Trust.

Dorothy is a member of the ACT Writers Centre and has attended many of their workshops. She also attended a writers course run by The Continuing Education Centre at the Australian National University. This is her first book.

About the Artist

Isla Patterson, a traditional watercolour artist, was born in South Australia and studied art with Trevor Clare and watercolours with Ruth Tuck. She lived in Washington DC for three years continuing her studies of watercolour and pastel portraiture and held her first solo exhibition. Isla settled in Canberra in 1979, developing her art especially in watercolours, travelling in Australia & overseas. She has won numerous awards and held well over 20 solo exhibitions and has paintings in many overseas countries as well as in Australia.

Isla belongs to ASOC (Artist Society of Canberra), The Queanbeyan Art Society, AIM (Art in Miniature), and is a signatory member of AGRA (Australian Guild of Realist Artists).

Awards in 2016 include The John Briscoe Award at Cooma Regional Gallery, Best in Show, Traditional, at the Lions Club Exhibition at Jindabyne and Best in Show, Molonglo Exhibition, Queanbeyan Art Society.

She has published articles in the *Australian Artist* Magazine, Antarctic in 2015 and Safari in 2016.

Commissions include paintings for Jason placemats, *The Canberra Times* building and international model buildings at Cockington Green ACT.

Introduction

Memorial to Australians who fell on French soil 1914–1918. Embassy of France (2016)

Canberra is a multicultural city of many facets. To many people, Canberra is merely the seat of the Federal Government—a city populated by politicians and public servants. Others think of it as the site of the Australian War Memorial, the National Gallery, Parliament House and other national institutions. However, as the nation's capital, it is home to nearly 100 overseas diplomatic missions with a large diplomatic community.

These diplomatic missions, known as Embassies or High Commissions, have been established to facilitate formal relationships between Australia and their home countries. The large diplomatic community gives Australians an informal insight into the culture and customs of these nations' homelands.

Since ancient times, trusted envoys have traditionally carried on communication between nations. In the Middle Ages, monks and priests were used for this service. Heralds were also used as ambassadors between different courts and every noble had his own herald. The profession of diplomacy can be traced back to the 15th century when the Italians began to appoint permanent ambassadors. However, the modern diplomatic corps owes its origins to the French when, after the Congress of Vienna in 1815, the rules and protocols of diplomacy were established.

Most diplomatic missions in Canberra are known as Embassies, headed by an Ambassador. The mission of countries which are members of the British Commonwealth are called High Commissions with a High Commissioner as their senior diplomat. Diplomatic appointments are usually for three to four years but many diplomats stay much longer. The longest serving ambassador or high commissioner is known as the Dean of the Diplomatic Corps. The order of precedence among the heads of diplomatic missions relates to the date that they first present their credentials to the Governor-General.

The work of the diplomatic missions is varied but includes trade, defence, immigration, cultural affairs and consular matters such as the issuing of visas. Some missions have large staff numbers including those locally engaged, while others only have a small representation. As well as the embassies in Canberra, many countries maintain consulates in the state capitals.

The first diplomatic mission was established in Canberra in 1936 when the United Kingdom appointed their first high commissioner to Australia. A year later Canada sent a representative and the United States followed in 1939.

When the United States Embassy was built in the 1940s in the form of a southern mansion, it started a trend for overseas missions to reflect the architectural style of their country. The National Capital Development Commission, who had the overall responsibility for the city's planning, encouraged other countries to construct buildings representative of traditional designs of their homeland. In 1958, when the National Capital Development Commission evolved into the National Capital Planning Authority and later to the National Capital Authority, this policy was continued. The distinctive national architectural pattern of many missions is fairly unique to Australia and is a great tourist attraction. The overseas chanceries (the office section of the embassy) and residences of the ambassadors are some of the treasures of Canberra. Some embassies have the official residence of their head of mission within the embassy grounds, while others are in separate locations.

Predominantly located in three Canberran suburbs of Yarralumla, Deakin and O'Malley, the embassies are easily identified by their distinctive architecture as well as their national flag being prominently displayed. Members of the European Union (EU) fly two flags—their national flag and that of the EU (a circle of gold stars on a blue background). Members of the Association of Southeast Asian Nations (ASEAN) also fly two flags, their national flag and the ASEAN flag. The colours of the ASEAN flag are blue representing peace and stability, red for courage and dynamism, white for purity and yellow for prosperity.

The conduct of official business at the embassies is generally limited to working hours but many also participate in open days for charity while others have special cultural performances that are open to the public. These include musical performances, special dance and food days, as well as art exhibitions. Some embassies have opened the gardens of their residences as part of The Open Garden Scheme. Missions celebrate their national days in various ways with many local Canberrans attending. The embassies are well represented at the National Multicultural Festival, which is held in Canberra in February each year. The Festival includes art exhibitions, theatre and concerts, as well as ethnic food outlets and dance performances. Windows to the World, a program originally started in 2013 as part of Canberra's centennial celebrations, is presented every two years in September. This program is an opportunity for the public to visit various embassies and be introduced to other countries' culture.

Embassies are further represented in a unique manner with the International Flag Display in Canberra's Parliamentary Zone. Situated in Commonwealth Place on the edge of Lake Burley Griffin, the flags represent those nations who maintain a diplomatic presence in the national capital. The flags are set in two rows of twelve metre flagpoles, fly 24 hours a day and are floodlit at night. A plaque at the base of the flagpole identifies the flags, which are maintained by the National Capital Authority. Sir William Deane, then Governor-General, launched the Flag Display on Australia Day 26 January 1999.

A popular tourist attraction in Canberra is the Cockington Green model village, which has an international section. Miniature buildings representing different countries are sponsored by various embassies.

This book examines 36 embassies and high commissions, each accompanied by illustrations. Most of these embassies showcase the diverse architecture of their countries. In addition, all foreign embassies and high commissions accredited to Australia and resident in Canberra are listed as an annex, along with their addresses.

Courtyard of the Royal Thai Embassy.
(2003)

Belgium

The Embassy of the Kingdom of Belgium's diplomatic links with Australia go back to the 1850s when a Consulate-General's office was opened in the colony of New South Wales. At this time Belgian wool-buying firms set up offices in Sydney opening the European market for Australian wool.

The Chancery, built in 1962, is a purely functional building. However, the Ambassador's residence, built two years earlier and located on the same grounds, is typical of architecture in Belgium. The building, designed by Sydney architects Fowell, Mansfield and Maclurcan, is a combination of modern and Flemish design. The windows with small panel glass and shutters are typically Flemish. Shutters are widely used in Belgium to protect against the cold winters and summer sun but at the Embassy they are purely decorative.

Belgium's National Day is 21 July. It commemorates that day in 1883 when the first King of Belgium, King Leopold 1, ascended the throne after the country's independence from the Netherlands. The day is celebrated in Brussels, the nation's capital, with a church service, attended by the Royal Family. The Te Deum (hymn of praise to God) is sung. In the afternoon there is a military parade reviewed by the King. A fireworks display is held in the evening. Similar ceremonies are held all over Belgium. In Australia, citizens of Belgian descent have individual celebrations.

Belgium was a founding member of the European Economic Community in 1958, later known as the European Union. Brussels, is home to the EU and The North Atlantic Treaty Organization (NATO).

As well as strong economic and trade relationships between Australia and Belgium, there are enduring historical ties from World War 1. The Australian Government has established a Western Front Interpretive Trail in both Belgium and France to honour the more than 290,000 Australians who served on the Front.

Belgium's Coat of Arms is represented by a golden lion featured on a black shield with the royal crown on top. The motto *L'union Fait La Force* (unity makes strength) is written on a ribbon below. Directly behind the shield are crossed sceptres.

The Belgian flag, flying next to the EU flag, has three coloured vertical stripes: black representing the shield, gold for the lion and red for the lions claws and tongue.

Residence, Embassy of Belgium (2016)

Bosnia and Herzegovina

Bosnia and Herzegovina is an European country on the Balkan Peninsula. It is bordered by Croatia, Serbia, and Montenegro

The Embassy of Bosnia and Herzegovina is located in the much newer Embassy area of Deakin. Formerly a constituent member of the Socialist Federal Republic of Yugoslavia, Bosnia and Herzegovina declared their sovereignty in October 1991 and followed this with a referendum in 1992 which endorsed the country's independence. Australia recognised Bosnia and Herzegovina in 1992 soon after the country became independent. The country established resident diplomatic representation in Australia in 1994 with a Chargé d'Affaires, the first Ambassador arriving in 2000.

Bosnia and Herzegovina Embassy sketch (2002)

The Chancery in Deakin was built in 2000. Neighbours include the Embassies of Hungary, Cyprus, Fiji, Timor-Leste, Brunei Darussalam, Mauritius, Afghanistan, Solomon Islands and Botswana. The building was designed by Nihad Handzic, an architect from Sarajevo now living in Sydney, while Anthony Mikulic, a Canberra architect, completed the project and construction plan. The building features the traditional Bosnian and Herzegovinian style architecture with a protruding top floor and a square castle roof. The building was officially opened on 14 June 2001 by Mr Ivica Misic then Deputy Foreign Minister of Bosnia/Herzegovina.

The National Day, also known as Statehood day, is celebrated on 25 November. On that day in 1943, the anti-fascist council of the National Liberation of Yugoslavia re-established Bosnia and Herzegovina as a republic within the Yugoslavian Federation. Bosniaks, Serbs and Croats were to be afforded equal community status.

Independence Day is celebrated on the 1st of March each year with a public holiday. It marks the independence of Bosnia/Herzegovina from the Socialist Federal Republic of Yugoslavia in 1992.

The National flag was promulgated in February

Canberra's Embassies

Bosnia and Herzegovina Embassy (2002)

1998. The flag has a medium blue background, a yellow triangle, seven white stars and two half stars. The blue background and white stars represent Europe while the yellow, the colour of the sun, symbolises hope. The triangle stands for the three ethnic groups in Bosnia /Herzegovina –Bosniaks, Croats and Serbs. The colours –white, blue and yellow are often associated with neutrality and peace, and traditionally are linked with Bosnia. The flag symbolizes that Bosnia and Herzegovina belong to the European democratic community.

Botswana

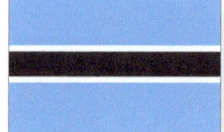

The Republic of Botswana is a landlocked nation in the middle of Southern Africa. It is bordered by Namibia, Zambia, Zimbabwe and South Africa. The Kalahari Desert occupies the western part of the country.

The official opening of the Chancery of the High Commission of Botswana took place on 17 June 2009. It was jointly opened by the former Minister of Foreign Affairs and International Co-operation of Botswana, Mr.Phandu Tombole Chaha Skelemani, and the former Minister for Foreign Affairs of Australia, Mr. Stephen Smith.

The building, which has won many architectural awards, reflects the classical public buildings of the British colonial era and the traditional decorated huts of the Tswana people. The feature brick patterning is derivative of traditional Botswana cultural crafts such as the famous Botswanan baskets. Inside the building there are large photomural artworks depicting animals which are significant to the people of Botswana. The elephant, lion and cheetah have a special place in tribal culture and each is representative of a major tribe of a specific region. Of special interest is the internal garden as it is typical of the Botswana geography. The open sandy spaces of the grassland and savannas of the Kalahari Desert are represented at the bottom of the garden. This gives way to the upper lush area of irrigated grass and trees of the eastern veld and northern region of Botswana.

The architects for the building were the firm of Guida Moseley Brown from Botswana while the builders were Kell and Rigby.

Botswana's national day is celebrated on September 30. It marks the date in 1966 when Botswana became

Botswana basket weaving (2016)

Botswana Embassy (2016)

independent from Great Britain. Since 1885 the region had been a British colony called the Bechuanaland protectorate. The day is marked by colourful festivities, songs by choir groups, dance (Borankana) and traditional cuisine. In villages the local community congregates at the Kgotia or public meeting place. In Canberra there is an official reception.

The national flag is designed with a blue background, and a large black stripe bordered by two white stripes. The blue is for the water, needed for agriculture, and the survival of Botswana. It also alludes to the motto on the coat of arms- *Pula*, meaning 'Let there be rain' in the national language. The black stripe with the white frame illustrates the peace and harmony between the people of African and European descent who live in Botswana.

Brazil

Brazil is the fifth largest country in the world, both in area and population. It is also the largest Portuguese speaking country. Brazil shares its border with every other South American country except Chile and Ecuador.

In July 1945 Australia opened a Legation in Rio de Janeiro, the old Capital of Brazil. The Brazilian Legation in Australia was opened the following year. In November 1959 it was upgraded to the Embassy of the Federative Republic of Brazil. The current Embassy in Yarralumla was built in the late eighties. It is a modern building with a wonderful view over Lake Burley Griffen.

The Ambassador's residence is not in the same location but is in the near-by suburb of Forrest. Known as Rofe House, it has an interesting history. Mr Thomas Rofe, a wealthy Sydney businessman and philanthropist, built the house as his country residence in 1927. That was the year that Canberra became the home of Australia's Federal Parliament. The house was acquired by the Brazilian Embassy in 1960.

Brazil's National Day, also known as Independence Day, is celebrated on 7 September. It commemorates the day in 1822 when Brazil claimed independence from Portugal. It is celebrated with 'banners, balloons and streamers' and fireworks at night. A military parade takes place in the presence of the President of Brazil. Concerts are held in Brasilia, the Capital. In Canberra the Embassy holds a reception.

While Independence Day is the most important public holiday, Brazil is also famous for its Carnival, a four-day extravaganza which is held in February.

Residence entrance detail (2001)

Embassy of Brazil (2016)

Brazil's colourful flag flying in the front of the Embassy, designed by Raimundo Teixeira Mendes, was officially adopted in 1889. It was modified to include newly created states. It features a blue circle globe with 27 white stars (originally 21), each star representing a specific state plus one for the Federal District. Spanning the globe is a curved band with the words of the national motto *Ordem e Progresso* (Order and Progress). The blue globe is placed on a gold diamond which in turn sits on a green background.

High Commission of Canada

Canada High Commission (2016)

The Chancery of the High Commission of Canada was officially opened on January 1964 by the then Prime Minister of Australia Sir Robert Menzies. Prior to this the Canadian Mission had operated for 23 years from Casey House in State Circle, the former home of Lord Casey.

The Chancery, built on classic lines, was designed by Mathers and Haldenby of Toronto, Canada. In 1994 a second wing was built at the rear of the building. Canadian timbers were used extensively throughout the building, including birch, rock, maple and pine. The roof is sheathed in copper and the eaves are made of Canadian red cedar.

A feature of the Chancery is the Canadian totem pole near the main entrance. Made for the World Expo, held in Brisbane in 1988, it is the work of an Haida Nation (First Nations) artist from the Queen Charlotte Islands off the coast of British Columbia. 600 hours of work were involved in carving this sculpture from a single red cedar trunk.

In 1868, the Governor General Lord Monck signed a proclamation encouraging Canadians to unite under a new Federation, in which the four separate provinces of Nova Scotia, New Brunswick, Ontario and Quebec became the Dominion of Canada. Originally known as Dominion Day, the name was changed to Canada Day in 1982 and each year is celebrated on 1 July.

Canada and Australia have had a tradition of exchanging gifts. In Canberra these gifts include the Senate President's chair in both old

Entrance, Canada High Commission (2015)

Parliament House in 1927 and the new Parliament House in 1988. In 1955 a flagpole made from a single spar of Douglas Fir from British Columbia was presented. It was erected on the shores of lake Burley Griffin at Regatta Point. Each year on Canada Day, the distinctive red maple leaf flag is flown from the flagpole.

Speakers Square, another gift of the Canadian Government, marked Australia's Centenary of Federation in 2001. The ten metre square granite work set in Commonwealth Place was designed by leading Canadian artist John McEwen. This work depicts the night skies of the northern and southern hemispheres, and represents the shared experiences of people of all nations, living together as one under the heavens.

The Canadian National flag, sometimes referred to as the maple leaf flag, was proclaimed into law on 15 February 1965. It is a red flag, in the centre of which is a white square with a single red maple leaf. Red and white have been the national colours of Canada since 1921.

China

Chinese Embassy roof designs (2003)

The Embassy of the Peoples' Republic of China is situated near the shores of Lake Burley Griffin. With distinctive Chinese architecture, the Embassy consists of a large administrative building, the Ambassador's Residence and staff quarters, all of which are located in one large security compound.

Behind the administrative building, between the Ambassador's residence and the staff quarters, lies a garden which embraces an ornamental lake, a zig-zag bridge and rockeries. In addition, internal gardens exist in the residence and the administrative building with an ornamental pond, stalagmite rocks and piled stones.

A pair of white marble lions is located in front of the chancellery as is the usual Chinese practice. Traditional Chinese golden glazed tiles are used for the roofs of most of the buildings while peacock blue glazed tiles cover the corridors and pavilions.

The China Guang Architectural Design Institute was one of the original architects, the building being finalized by Wulu and Partners of Hong Kong. The Australian building company, Leighton carried out the main structural and building work. The foundation stone laying ceremony took place in November 1988 in the presence of the Chinese Premier Li Peng. Construction began in November 1988 and was completed in July 1990.

The Chinese National Day is celebrated on October 1st. The day commemorates the founding of the Peoples' Republic of China in 1949, and was formally promulgated the following day by a special resolution of the government. The day was originally celebrated with a military review and parade but nowadays the parades take place every 5 or 10 years.

Chinese Embassy grand entrance (2003)

Other activities like flag raising ceremonies, fireworks, and art and calligraphy exhibitions are held on the day.

The Chinese flag, proudly flying in front of the Embassy, was officially adopted at the same date as the National Day – 1 October 1949. The flag was first flown on this date in Tiananmen Square in Beijing. The flag has a red background with one large gold star and four smaller stars in the top left hand corner. The stars each have five points. The red of the flag symbolizes revolution, the large star represents the Communist Party of China and the smaller stars represent the people.

Croatia

Hidden within the walls of the beautiful Embassy of the Republic of Croatia is a secret not known to many outside the Croatian community. Unlike other countries which have their embassies built and financed by their governments, the Croatian Embassy was constructed with voluntary contributions, both manual and financial, from the Australian Croatian community.

For most of its history Croatia was part of the Hungarian kingdom but in 1918 it was incorporated into the Kingdom of the Serbs, Croats, and Slovenes, which became Yugoslavia in 1929. After the Second World War and with the collapse of communism in Eastern Europe in 1989, nationalistic fervor and appeal for democracy catalysed the breakup of the Yugoslav federation as individual republics agitated for their independence. Croatia declared its independence in 1991 but this resulted in conflict with the Yugoslav communist army dominated by the Serbs, which was only resolved in January 1992 with the deployment of a United Nations peacekeeping force.

Australia recognised Croatia in January 1992 shortly after its declaration of independence and diplomatic relations were established the following month.

Construction of the Embassy building began in 1994 and such was the dedication and industry of the Croatian community it was completed by early 1995. Near the front entrance is the foundation stone with the following dedication—'As a gift to the Republic of Croatia from the Croatian community of Australia'. The blessing of the land upon which the Croatian Embassy will be built. Officially opened in June 1995 by the first President of Croatia, Dr Franjo Tudjman, the building commands a majestic vista from the heights of O'Malley.

Designed by Antony Mikulic, a Canberran architect of Croatian descent, the building was

Croatian Embassy tower (2001)

and to the remembrance of Croatian migrants of the roots of their being'.

Many Croatian works of art are displayed both inside the building and in the attractive garden. One sculpture set in the garden by Marijan Bakic portrays an image of a woman's form as Mother Croatia, providing comfort to all children of her homeland and represents over 1300 years of Croatian history.

The Croatian National Day (Statehood Day), is observed on 25 June each year celebrating the anniversary of the country's independence in 1991. The Embassy hosts a reception on this day to mark the occasion. In Croatia it is a public holiday with the government holding a military parade in the capital Zagreb.

The Croatian flag, adopted in December 1990, features a tricolor of red white and blue representing the Kingdom of Croatia, Slavonia and Dalmatia with the coat of arms in the centre. It flies next to the European Union flag, Croatia being admitted in July 2013.

inspired by the historic castles from the continental part of Croatia. A former ambassador Dr Jozo Meter described it as a 'lighthouse on a hilltop, standing witness to the steadfastness of the Croatian people

Delegation of the European Union

The European Union (EU) is represented in Australia by a Delegation in Canberra which was established in 1981. The Delegation has full diplomatic privileges and immunities with the Head of Delegation accorded full ambassadorial status in Australia. The Delegation is responsible for the conduct of official relations between the European Union and Australia.

The Chancery of the Delegation and the Ambassador's residence are situated on the same site in Yarralumla. Built in 1988 the Chancery is a very open and bright building. Roses and flower beds make an attractive display at the front entrance. The architects were Anthony Cooper and Associates of Canberra.

The EU is a political and economic integration process of 28 European countries with more than 500 million citizens which collectively comprise the world's largest economy. Australia has strong links with the EU as diplomatic relations were established in 1952. Bilateral relations will be further enhanced by a new bilateral treaty, the EU-Australia Framework Agreement. The Delegation works closely with the diplomatic missions of the EU member states in representing the EU as a whole in Australia.

The National Day of the EU is 9 May. Known as Europe Day it is an annual celebration of peace and unity. Robert Schuman, the then French Foreign Minister, realised that there could never be unity in Europe without reconciliation with Germany. He drew up the Schuman Declaration on May 9th 1950 which was the basis for the European Coal and Steal Community which placed the production of coal and steel of France, Germany, Italy, Belgium, the Netherlands and Luxembourg under one common high authority. This organisation grew to be the European Economic Community in 1958, then the European Union in 1993. In the intervening years other countries joined until today the EU has achieved its current membership of 28.

The flag of the European Union, which was adopted in 1985, features a circle of 12 gold stars

Entrance to the EU Delegation (2001).

on a blue background. The number of stars is fixed and does not reflect the number of states in the EU. The stars stand for the ideals of unity, solidarity and harmony among the peoples of Europe.

In 2012 the EU was awarded the Nobel Peace Prize for advancing the causes of peace, reconciliation, democracy, and human rights in Europe.

Fiji

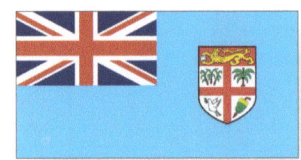

The Dutch explorer and navigator, Abel Tasman, accidentally discovered Fiji in 1643. British Captain, James Cook, also sailed through the islands in 1774, but credit for the first European exploration goes to Captain William Bligh. The Republic of Fiji is a group of 331 beautiful islands and 520 islets, of which only about 100 are inhabited. The indigenous name for the islands is Viti meaning 'east' or 'sunrise'. The two main islands are Viti Levu and Vanua Levu which account for 87% of the population. The Capital is Suva situated on the south east of Viti Levu. Fiji has the most advanced economy of the Pacific islands, and is a renowned tourist destination.

The Chancery of the High Commission of Fiji is located in the diplomatic enclave of Deakin. Opened in 1997, the main building is a modern structure with a very high sloping tiled roof, in keeping with the manner of traditional Fiji huts, known as *bure*, although these have thatched roofs. There is a series of smaller buildings at the side of the chancery, all with traditional style architecture. Visitors to the chancery are heralded with the beating of the lali, which is a traditional drum-like apparatus, fashioned from a hollowed out tree trunk.

The Chancery plays custodian to a fine collection of artefacts, ranging from traditional wooden spears, clubs, finely woven mats and fans to modern coconut timber furniture which is proudly displayed throughout the Chancery. The Chancery's archive also boasts its own collection of newspapers dating back to the pre-cession period and photographs from as far back as the Girmitya period of Indian indentured labour of the late 1800s.

The National Day of Fiji is celebrated on October 10th. Known as Fiji Day it is the anniversary of Fiji's independence from British colonial rule in 1970. October 10th is also the date in 1874 when Fiji was ceded to the United Kingdom.

Fiji's Coat of Arms consists of the images of two Fijian warriors on either side of a shield and the motto *Rerevaka na Kalou ka Doka na Tui* meaning 'Fear God and honour the Queen' at the bottom. Above the shield is a Fijian outrigger canoe. On the top of the shield itself is a golden lion above a St George cross. Sugar cane, a coconut palm, and a bunch of bananas, all grown in Fiji, plus a dove of

High Commission of Fiji. (2002)

peace are placed in the four quarters around the cross.

Fiji's current National flag flew for the first time on the day independence was declared in 1970. The flag features the Union Jack in the top left hand corner and the shield from Fiji's Coat of Arms on a pale blue background.

Finland and Estonia

Finland established diplomatic relations with Australia in 1919 when a Consulate opened in Sydney. In 1966 an Embassy was established in Canberra but it was 1978 before an official Chancery and Ambassador's residence was built on the present site. After twenty years the Chancery became too crowded and a new building was required. An architectural competition was held to design a new Chancery which resulted in the outstanding modern building known as the Ilmarinen. The name Ilmarinen is originally the name of the blacksmith hero of the Finnish epic Kalevala.

The architect was Vesa Huttunen who was inspired by an armoured vessel of the Finnish Navy also named *Ilmarinen*, a ship sunk during the Second World War. The striking facade of the building is wholly made of glass to resemble a ship with the internal offices lined up along the side like cabins. The rear wall is clad internally and externally with stainless steel and protruding strip windows.

The building has been greatly admired by architects throughout Australia and in 2003 was recognised with a special architectural award from the Royal Australian Institute of Architects. A special feature of the Chancery is the real Finnish sauna at the back of the building.

In 2015, Finland leased part of the building to its neighbour Estonia and it now houses the Embassy of Estonia in Canberra.

The national day of Finland is December 6, commemorating the date in 1917 when Finland declared its independence. After centuries as part of Sweden, Finland became an autonomous Grand Duchy of the Russian Empire in 1809. Following the Bolshevik coup d'état in November 1917 Finland declared its full independence of Russia.

Numerous formal and informal events occur on this day but the highlight occurs in the evening when the President holds an Independence Day Reception. The event is broadcast on national TV. A family tradition on Independence Day is to light two candles in the windows of their homes in the evening.

Three flags fly outside the Chancery, the National Flags of Finland and Estonia and the flag of the

European Union (EU) as both countries are member states of the EU. The National Flag of Finland features a blue cross on a white background. The blue is said to represent the country's thousands of lakes and the sky while the white denotes the snow that covers the land in winter. The blue cross has also represented Christianity. The Finnish flag was made official by a law enacted on May 29, 1918, less than six months after independence. Finland joined the EU in 1995 and Estonia joined in 2004.

On the Estonian flag, blue represents the reflection of the sky in the lakes and the sea, symbolizing endurance – 'until the skies last'; black stands for the earth that feeds its people; white marks an aspiration towards light and purity.

Embassies of Finland and Estonia (2016)

France

The Embassy of France in Australia, situated in Yarralumla, was officially opened in November 1959. Diplomatic relations between France and Australia however go back to 1864 with a representative in Sydney.

Both the Chancery and the Ambassador's Residence were designed by the French architect M.J. Desmaret. The residence is set behind the Chancery on a crest and has a wonderful view of the surrounding countryside including Lake Burley Griffin and Parliament House.

In the grounds of the Embassy is a memorial erected by the French Government to honour the memory of the Australians who lost their lives in France during the First World War. It was unveiled on 28 July 1961 by The Right Honorable Robert Menzies, the then Prime Minister of Australia. Commemorative ceremonies are held at the memorial every Anzac Day and Remembrance Day.

The memorial is a stone masonry column fifteen feet high, designed by the French architect Desmaret. On top of the column is a sculpture, 'Winged Victory', in gilded bronze, the work of French sculptor Bizette-Lindet.

On the front of the column are the words *Aux Australiens Qui Sont Tombés Sur La Terre De France En Souvenir De Leur Sacrifice Pour La Liberté des Peuples 1914-1918* (To Those Australians Who Fell On French Soil In Memory of Their Sacrifice for the Freedom of All People). On the sides, the names of the battles on French soil and in which Australians were involved have been inscribed. Armentières, Fromelles, Hazebrouck, Pozières, Bullecourt, Amiens, Villers-Bretonneux, Dernancourt, Mont St Quentin, Somme, Hargicourt, Bellicourt.

Bastille Day is the National Day of France and is celebrated every year on July 14th. It commemorates the 1789 storming of the Bastille, a French prison, an event that initiated the French Revolution, but also the *Fête de la Fédération*, on 14 July 1790, a celebration one

Embassy of France entrance (2016)

year later to symbolize peace and of the unity of the French nation. The storming of the Bastille marked the end of the reign of Louis XVI, which eventually led to the creation of the First Republic, in 1792.

The French flag, known as the *Tricolore*, flies proudly outside the Embassy together with the flag of the European Union, of which France was a founding member in 1958.

Greece

Entrance steps Greek Embassy (2001)

The Embassy of the Hellenic Republic is easily recognized by its distinctive architecture. The Chancery and the adjacent Ambassador's residence, built in the early eighties, resemble well known buildings in Greece. The design was approved by the Greek Ministry of Public Works, in association with the architectural firm Bunning and Madden in Canberra. The marble used in the buildings was shipped from Greece, being excavated from the same quarries used by the ancient Athenians, for buildings such as the Parthenon and the Acropolis. The Doric columns surrounding the buildings are inspired by ancient Greek architecture. There is a taverna at the back which is popular for summer entertaining.

Greece was represented in Australia in the latter part of the 19th century and early 20th century by Honorary Consulates, the first Ambassador of Greece arriving in 1953. Formal Consulates are located in Melbourne, Sydney, Adelaide and Perth. Brisbane, Darwin and Hobart are represented by Honorary Consulates.

The Greek National Day or Independence Day is 25 March. It commemorates the start of the War of Greek Independence in 1821 after four centuries of Ottoman occupation. After early successes the revolution appeared to be failing but assistance came

Embassy of Greece (2001)

in Greece with a military parade in Athens, and many other and varying events. In towns across Greece schools hold flag parades. The children march in traditional Greek costume and carry Greek flags. In Canberra, the Ambassador hosts a formal reception in his residence. Greek communities all over Australia, especially in Melbourne which is known as the third largest 'Greek City' in the world, have their own celebrations.

The Greek National flag has nine alternating horizontal stripes of blue and white. A white cross on a blue background is in the top left hand corner. The cross represents the Greek religion, Eastern Orthodox Christianity. The cross also appears on the Greek Coat of Arms surrounded by a laurel wreath.

Greece joined the European Union in 1981.

from Great Britain, France and Russia. At the naval battle of Navarino the combined British, French and Russian forces destroyed an Ottoman-Egyptian fleet. The revolution ended in 1829 with the Treaty of Edirne establishing an independent Greek state. The revolution was the first successful national revolution of 19th century Europe. The day, a public holiday, is celebrated

Grecian urn

Hungary

Located in Central Europe, Hungary is bordered by Austria, Slovakia, Ukraine, Romania, Serbia, Croatia and Slovenia. Its Capital is Budapest. Hungary – a member of NATO and the European Union—established consular (1967) and diplomatic relations (1972) with Australia, and in 1975 the first ambassador was appointed to Canberra.

The Embassy complex, built in 1990 in the newer embassy area of Deakin, represents a typical Hungarian country house with an open arcade and arched windows. The main building contains the chancery and staff apartments. There are two other buildings in the complex; one is the Ambassador's residence while the other is the Millennium Hall, a multifunction centre as well as an art treasure. Within, a high painted wooden ceiling, the work of Hungarian artist Tibor Brada, contains panels, popular in the 17th century in the Calvinist churches in Hungary. They show important dates in Hungary's history, including the Rákóczi War of Independence of 1703-1711, the Revolution and War of Independence of 1848-1849, and the 1956 Revolution and War of Independence. Historic figures, including former kings, military leaders, artists, writers, and religious leaders can also be seen. Banners of different victorious battle troops are displayed on the walls of the Hall. Amongst the art works is a tapestry of Rembrandt's 'Night Watch', and—outside in the garden—a fountain statue, 'Temptation of Socrates' is the work of prize winning Hungarian sculptor Miklos Melcocco.

Sketch of the nine arches back view, Embassy of Hungary (2001)

Hungary's official state holiday of 20th August is celebrated throughout the country with fireworks, in memory of the foundation of the State and the State Founder, King Saint Stephen I. Other national days are

Nine arches back view, Embassy of Hungary (2001)

15th March, in memory of the 1848-49 Revolution and War of Independence and 23rd October, in memory of the 1956 Revolution and War of Independence

Two flags fly outside the Hungarian embassy, the national flag and the flag of the European Union. The flag of Hungary features three horizontal bands of equal width coloured red, white and green from top to bottom as the symbols of strength, fidelity and hope, respectively. The coat of arms of Hungary is a vertically divided shield design with a pointed base. The left field contains eight horizontal bars of red and silver. The right field has a red background and depicts a base of three green hills with a golden crown atop the higher central hill from which rises a silver patriarchal cross. The Holy Crown rests on top of the shield. Hungary joined the EU in 2004.

In 2016, the Hungarian Embassy was accredited under the 'ACT Smart Business Recycling' program of the ACT, as second accredited mission in Canberra after the U.S. Embassy.

High Commission of India

Diplomatic relations between the Republic of India and Australia were established in 1944, the first High Commissioner being appointed in 1946. The Chancery, which opened in 1981, was designed by Bunning and Madden, architects in Canberra. The building was formally opened by Mrs Indira Gandhi, former prime minister of India, in October 1981.

The Chancery is a traditional Indian building, inspired by Mughal architecture. The building is designed as a single two storey structure around a central internal space. The tiered roof over the central area culminates with a golden Kalash, a symbol of India, and the crowning feature. A deep covered veranda with white ornamental pillars surrounds the perimeter of the building. A feature of the Chancery site is the iron gate which opens on to two parallel flights of stairs leading down to the front door. Between the stairs, a tiered waterfall flows into a shallow moat, giving an impression of a floating Chancery building. The garden is terraced and follows the features of Mughal gardens of Kashmir.

India celebrates two National Days, Independence Day and Republic Day. 15 August commemorates the date in 1947 when India, under the leadership of Mahatma Gandhi, obtained its independence from Great Britain. On this date the former British Indian Empire was divided into two countries, India and Pakistan. The day is a national holiday and is celebrated with flag raising ceremonies and cultural ceremonies all over India. India's President addresses the nation on the eve of Independence day. The Prime minister gives a speech to the nation at the Red Fort in Delhi. This tradition started with India's first Prime Minister,

Sketch of the High Commission of India (2001)

High Commission of India (2001)

Pandit Nehru, giving his famous 'Tryst with destiny' speech in 1947.

In Canberra after a flag raising in the morning, the High Commissioner reads the President's message. There is a reception at the Embassy in the evening.

Republic day is commemorated on the 26th of January. It is a public holiday and marks the day in 1950 when India's constitution came into force. A grand military parade is held in New Delhi, the capital, and flag raising ceremonies take place across the country. In Canberra there is a similar flag raising ceremony.

India's National flag is a horizontal tricolour of saffron, white and green, with a navy blue wheel in the centre of the white band. The saffron stands for courage and sacrifice, the white for purity and truth, and the green for faith and fertility. The wheel represents the dharma chakra and symbolises the wheel of law.

Indonesia

Music room, Indonesian Embassy (2003)

The Republic of Indonesia is an archipelago of more than 17,000 islands, situated between Asia and Australia. The population of Indonesia exceeds 250 million and with more than 200 ethnic groups speaking 583 languages and dialects, the nation is a melting pot of cultures and customs.

General Suharto, the former President of Indonesia, officially opened the Embassy on 7 February 1972, during a four-day official visit to Australia, the event commemorated by the planting of an Arizona Cyprus.

Initially the Chancery consisted of a main office block and the cultural centre (*Balai Budaya*) but was extended in the 1980s to include an annex and a second building (*Balai Kartini*). The original office block of the Chancery was designed by George Holland and the later additions by Leith Bartlett and Partners. All the buildings were modelled on typical Indonesian government office blocks of that era.

The Embassy's most distinctive feature is the series of hand-carved stone Balinese sculptures on the steps leading to the *Balai Budaya*. The statues represent personalities from two ancient Hindu legends that have been adopted by the Indonesian people for centuries. Although the Indonesians (except the Balinese) renounced Hinduism in the 16th century, these Hindu stories have an important place in Indonesian culture.

At the top of the ornamental stairs is a replica of a Balinese temple gate, leading to a terrace with more sculptures and the *Balai Budaya*. This structure is built in the form of a traditional Javanese *pendopo* (or pavilion) and houses a collection of Indonesian arts and crafts as well as musical instruments , including a Gamelan orchestra. The *pendopo* is traditionally open on all sides, however this building has been adapted to the Canberra climate, and has glass walls. The *pendopo* is surrounded by a pond with fountains and small statues.

Another building at the rear is the *Balai Kartini*, a venue for all official occasions. It has been named in honour of Raden Ajeng Kartini (1879-1904), a national figure and one of the best known pioneers of the Indonesian Woman's Movement.

The Indonesian flag is a horizontal bicolour of red and white. The red symbolizes human bravery and the white represents the human spirit. Beside it is the ASEAN flag, Indonesia being a foundation member of ASEAN when it was formed in 1967.

The coat of arms of Indonesia is called Garuda Pancasila. The main part is the gold *Garuda* (a mythical golden eagle) with a shield on its chest and a scroll gripped by its leg. The *Garuda* symbolizes strength and power, while the gold colour symbolizes greatness and glory.

Indonesian Embassy (2016)

Hand carved Balinese sculpture on the steps leading to the cultural centre (2003)

Ireland

Sketch of the Embassy of Ireland entrance (2001)

A picture postcard scene of a tranquil rural property is the image projected by the Chancery of the Embassy of Ireland. Modelled on the lines of an Irish farmhouse with typical external white-washed walls, its brown-tiled roof reminds one of the traditional thatching of such buildings in Ireland. The current diplomatic mission's property was designed by Philip Cox and Partners, Canberra architects, with both the Chancery and the Residence having won several architectural awards. The Embassy has also been listed on the Register of Significant 20th Century Architecture.

Ireland and Australia established diplomatic relations in 1946 when the first Ambassador arrived, with the Chancery located in Civic for many years. The current Chancery was built in 1980 and officially opened later that year by the Ambassador F. O'Riordan. A new Residence on the same site was completed in 2003.

Ireland's National Day is observed on the 17 March each year, the feast day of Saint Patrick, Patron Saint of the Nation. St Patrick is credited with bringing Christianity to Ireland in the 5th century AD. A public holiday, it is commemorated in Ireland with parades in the cities, towns and villages and the wearing of the green. It has become a global celebration of what it means to be Irish, the New York parades being an example. St Patrick's Day is also widely observed in Australia as many people can trace their Irish forebears. It is estimated that 30 per cent of Australians have Irish heritage.

The National flag of Ireland is a tricolour of green, white and orange vertical stripes. The green represents the Gaelic and Anglo-Norman element in the population, while the orange represents the Protestant tradition. The white signifies a lasting peace between the Irish Protestant and Irish Catholic. The first known use of the flag was in the revolutionary year of 1848, when Thomas Francis Meagher used it as an emblem of the

Embassy of Ireland entrance (2001)

Young Ireland movement. However, it was not until the Easter Rising in 1916, when it was raised above the General Post Office in Dublin, that the tricolour came to be regarded as the national flag.

The Coat of Arms of Ireland features a gold harp with silver strings on an azure field. The model for the representation of the heraldic harp is the fourteenth century 'Brian Boru' harp now preserved in the Museum of Trinity College, Dublin.

In 1973 Ireland joined the European Economic Community which became the European Union in 1993.

Italy

Statue in the residence (2016)

Italy established Diplomatic Relations with Australia in 1946, just after the end of the 2nd World War. The present Chancery and the adjacent Ambassador's residence, were built in 1966-67, close to the Australian Prime Minister's residence, the Lodge.

Designed by the Italian Ministry of Public Works in Rome, the construction was supervised by the Canberra architect Enrico Taglietti. The residence was built like a *Villa Romana* with two internal courtyards similar to the Roman villas of 2000 years ago. The courtyards are set with greenery, floral and ornamental waters, surrounded and paved by Italian tiles. Various rooms were laid out around the courtyard.

The Chancery and residence were officially opened in September 1967, by the then President of Italy, Giuseppi Saragat and his Prime Minister Amintore Fanfani who were visiting Australia at that time.

Italy's National Day, Republic Day, is celebrated on 2nd June. Known in Italy as *Festa della Repubblica* (Festival of the Republic), it marks the date in 1946 when Italians voted to abolish the monarchy and become a republic. It was the first time that Italian women were allowed to vote. A new constitution was written for the country, taking effect on 1 January 1948 when Italy officially became the Italian Republic. A public holiday, it is celebrated with military parades and official ceremonies, including the

Italian Embassy (2016)

laying of a wreath on the Tomb of the Unknown Soldier inside the *Altare della Patria* (Altar of the Fatherland) in Rome. In Canberra the ambassador holds a reception.

The Italian flag is a tricolour of green, white and red vertical stripes. The colours were first adopted by the military in 1796 with arms and crown in the centre. When Italy became a republic it dispensed with the coat of arms and crown and adopted the tricolour. The green is said to represent the colours of the landscape, the white the snow of the mountains and the red represents the blood shed by soldiers. Italy was a foundation member of The European Economic Community in 1958, which later became the European Union.

In the garden of the Chancery there is a sculpture commemorating young workers, by famous Italian artist Mario Negri. (1916-1987).

Japan

The Embassy garden is styled in the traditional Japanese manner, featuring rocks, a stone bridge, lanterns, a pond, streams and a pagoda. The stone lanterns, which are ornamental as well as practical, were brought from Japan. Two bronze lanterns in the garden were donated to the Embassy by the Missionary Sisters of the Sacred Heart in Melbourne in November 1980. Another feature of the garden is the tea-house. Regarded as an essential component of a Japanese garden, its main purpose is to enable visitors to rest and enjoy the view of the garden and its surroundings. The gardens were planned by the firm of Lida Zoen Jimusho of Tokyo, who sent one of their landscape architects to Canberra to lay out the gardens.

Prior to 1953, when the first Ambassador arrived, Japan was represented in Australia by several Consulates-General in Sydney and Melbourne. The first Chancery of the Embassy of Japan was located in Forrest, but in 1970 a new chancery was built on its present site in Yarralumla. The Chancery was designed to be in harmony with the Ambassador's residence which had been in 1961. While the buildings are made of reinforced concrete, they have many features of the wooden structures of older Japanese buildings, including pillars and handrails along the verandas.

Snow Lantern (2016)

The Japanese Embassy is associated with the Nara Candle Festival held each year in the Nara Peace Park. Situated in the Lennox Gardens on the shores of Lake Burley Griffin, the Nara Peace Park features a small Japanese themed garden. Canberra and Nara, the first Capital of Japan, are sister cities.

Every year, the Embassy of Japan celebrates His Majesty the Emperor's birthday as its National Day.

Canberra's Embassies

Residence Embassy of Japan (2007)

The national flag of Japan, flying in the front of the embassy, is white with a deep red disc in the centre. The flag, known as Hinomaru or circle of the sun, became the official national flag on August 13 1999.

High Commission of Malaysia

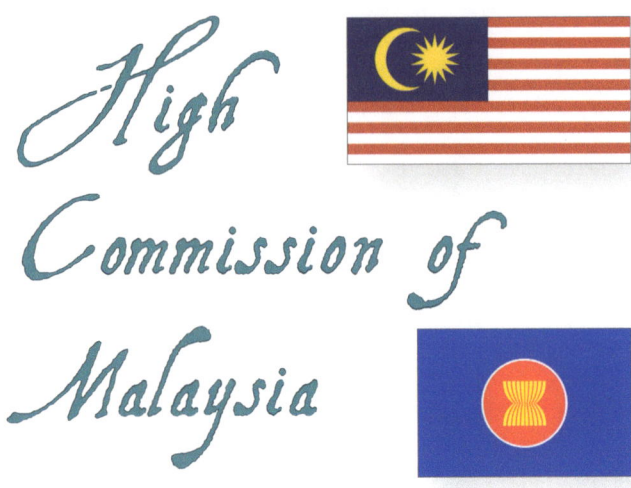

Malaysia started bilateral relations with Australia in August 1956 when the country, then known as the Federation of Malaya under British protection, established a Commission of the Federation of Malaya in Canberra, in preparation of its independence. A year later, Malaysia and Australia formally established diplomatic relations when the country achieved independence and sent its First High Commissioner to Australia, H.E. Gunn Lay Teik, who presented his credentials on 25 September 1957. In 1963 the Federation was renamed Malaysia. As well as all the Malay States this new Federation included Singapore and two areas in North Borneo - Sarawak and Sabah. Singapore left the Federation in 1965 to become a separate country.

The Chancery of the High Commission was built in 1984 and was officially opened by the 4th Prime Minister of Malaysia, Dr Mahathir bin Mohamad on 10 August of that year. The building is typical Malaysian architecture with *Minangkabau* roof style, a traditional design from the State of Negeri Sembilan. The flower motifs on the outside walls represent Malaysia's national flower, the *Bunga Raya* (red hibiscus). Inside the chancery cultural centre there is a display of Selangor pewter and Malaysian craft. These include traditional costumes, batik, pottery, Kelantan kites and Mengkuang artefacts. The building was designed in Malaysia.

Sketch of the High Commission of Malaysia (2002)

Malaysia's National Day is celebrated on 31 August each year. It marks the date when the country gained independence from British colonial rule. The day, a national holiday, is celebrated with parades and processions at Federal and State levels. The Malaysian flag is hoisted throughout the country. There is a

High Commission of Malaysia (2002)

variety of shows, exhibitions and other events. The parades are usually held in the morning and fireworks displays are held at night. In Canberra a reception is held at the Chancery or High Commissioner's residence.

The national flag of Malaysia consists of 14 horizontal red and white stripes. This represents the equal membership in the federation of the 13 component states as well as the Federal Territory. In the upper left hand corner is a yellow crescent and a yellow star on a dark blue background. The crescent is the symbol of Islam, Malaysia's official religion. The fourteen-point star represents the unity of the 13 States and the Federal Territory. The dark blue in the upper quarter stands for the unity of the Malaysian people. The yellow of the crescent and the star is the royal colour of the Malay rulers.

The other flag flying beside the national flag is the ASEAN flag. Malaysia was a founding member of ASEAN when it was formed in 1967.

Mexico

Although Australia and Mexico have had diplomatic relations since 1966 the current Embassy was not established until 1982. Designed by Mexican architect, Alfredo Terrazas de la Peña, the Embassy combines elements of both modern and traditional Mexico.

The modern is represented by the very clear, functional design of the Embassy. It is an open plan with plain white walls which blend into the surroundings. Traditional elements reflecting Mexico's long history include two columns or Mayan lintels. Two sculptured jaguars enhance the entrance of the Embassy; these animals were revered in Aztec mythology and were the symbol of both rulers and warriors.

One of the most iconic landmarks within the Embassy grounds is a replica of the Sun Stone or Aztec Calendar on the wall by the main gates. The original stone, which weighs 24.5 tons, is in the Museum of Anthropology in Mexico City. As well as a calendar, it is a narrative of Aztec time and history. It comprises a central disc and three outer rings. The Aztec time was measured in cycles of 20 days that moved in 13 different positions, that is, cycles of 260 days. The central disc displays an image of Tonatiuh, the Aztec god of the sun, who is also deeply related to war. Aztecs depicted Tonatiuh as a fair skinned god with blonde hair, just as the rays of the sun. He is sticking his tongue out, which is a sign of bravery, and the tongue is also a war dagger.

The symbols for the 20 Aztec days are represented in the first outer ring. The second outer ring indicates the four cardinal points and also the rays of the sun. The third outer ring is encircled by two fire snakes, these animals being important elements of ancient Mexican civilizations.

Fierce statue at the entrance. (2016)

Inside the Chancery there is a model of how the Aztec capital looked when the Spanish arrived in the early sixteenth century. Known as Tenochtitlan, it was probably the biggest city in the Western Hemisphere at the time with an estimated population of 250 thousand. It had over 70 temples including the

Canberra's Embassies

Embassy of Mexico featuring the Sun Stone (2016).

Templo Mayor which features in the model. This temple was devoted to the gods of rain and war, the two most important Aztec deities.

Mexico's National Day is 16 September celebrating the beginning of the Independence movement in 1810. On 15 September at 11pm, the *El Grito* ceremony (Shout of Independence) takes place throughout Mexico. In Mexico City the President appears on the balcony of the National Palace and repeats the 1810 rallying cry of Father Hidalgo who led Mexico to full independence.

The Mexican flag adopted in 1984 is a tricolor of green, white and red with the Coat of Arms, featuring an eagle holding a serpent, in the middle.

Myanmar

The Republic of the Union of Myanmar is a country in south-east Asia which was formerly known as Burma. The name was changed in June 1989. Myanmar is bordered by China in the north, in the east by Laos and Thailand, in the west by Bangladesh and India and by the Andaman Sea and the Bay of Bengal in the south. The capital, formerly Rangoon, is the planned city of Naypyidaw.

Diplomatic relations between Australia and Burma were formally established in 1953. The Chancery in Yarralumla was completed in 1988, previously the Embassy was located in Red Hill. As Myanmar is predominately a Buddhist country (89%), the official opening was performed by a Buddhist Monk who blessed the building a week before the Chancery was occupied. The morning ceremony was attended by Embassy staff and family members, who recited prayers and made offerings in accordance with Myanmar Buddhist traditions.

The Chancery is a two storey structure with a circular driveway around the flagpole, giving access to the building. Steel columns surrounding the building support distinctive steel lattice work, reminiscent of the woven construction of lattice screening in traditional houses in Myanmar. The extensive use of glass is a feature of the design, with floor to ceiling windows. The architects were Sam Lee, Stephenson and Turner in Victoria.

The country's National Day, or Independence Day, is one of the few non-religious holidays in Myanmar. The exact date of the National Day changes each year as it is based on the Lunar Calendar. There are 12 lunar months of 29 or 30 days each. This adds up to 354 days, so an extra make-up month is added every 2 to 3 years. The day commemorates the regaining of independence from Great Britain in 1948. In Myanmar there is a national holiday. In Canberra a morning flag raising ceremony is held at the Chancery, presided over by the Head of Mission and attended by Embassy staff. A reception for the diplomatic community is usually held as well as a function with the Myanmar community.

Myanmar Embassy (2015)

Myanmar's new flag was adopted on 21 October 2010. The flag is a horizontal tricolour with yellow, green and red stripes and a large white, five-pointed star in the middle of the flag. The yellow symbolises solidarity, the green peace, tranquillity, and vegetation, and the red, courage and decisiveness. The white star represents the union of the country.

Myanmar joined ASEAN in 1997.

Netherlands

The old Chancery (2003)

The Netherlands has had a long association with Australia. As far back as 1606, Dutch Mariner Willem Jansz, Captain of the *Duyfken*, landed on the Gulf of Carpentaria coast of Cape York Peninsula. His was the first known European contact with the Australian continent. The second recorded landing on Australian soil was that of Dirk Hartog on the west coast in 1616. In the remainder of the 17th century the Dutch explored much of the western coast of the continent which they called New Holland.

The first Dutch legation in Australia was formally established in November 1941. Baron F.C. van Aerssen was appointed first Minister for the Netherlands in Canberra in April 1942. In that same year, Australia's High Commissioner in London, S.M. Bruce, was accredited Australian Envoy to the Netherlands. The first Netherlands Ambassador accredited to Australia was P.D.E Teixeira de Mattos in 1951.

The first chancery, built in 1954-1955, with its distinctive half-moon shape, can be seen in the Embassy grounds. The new Chancery of the Kingdom of the Netherlands was built in 2012-2013; it is a very modern building designed by the Canberra firm of Phil Leeson Architects.

The chancery was officially opened on 26 February 2014 by the then Dutch Foreign Affairs Minister, Frans Timmermans, and Australian Senator, George Brandis..

A rectangular two-story building, it is very spacious internally and has been designed with optimum climate control. The east and west sides of the building are closed to prevent warming from the sun at the beginning and end of the day, and to reduce energy consumption. The offices, all with large double-glazed windows, are mainly

The new Netherlands Embassy (2016)

located on the north and south sides of the building. Solar panels and an underground water tank enhances the environmental design. Inside the building it is very bright. Ceiling lights adapt to the outside light and switch off automatically when the office is not being used.

The annual celebration of King's Day on 27 April is a national holiday, marking the King's birthday. The colour of the Royal family is orange. The streets of the cities become a sea of orange with children and many adults dressed in orange clothing. There are many fairs and musicians play at street markets. In Australia the embassy holds a reception.

Two flags are flying in front of the chancery, the national flag and that of the EU of which they were a founding member in 1958. The national flag with its bands of red, white and blue is one of the oldest flags in constant use, originating with William 1, Prince of Orange, in the latter half of the 16th century.

High Commission of New Zealand

The New Zealand High Commission Chancery is situated between the Canadian and the United Kingdom Chanceries in what is often called 'Old Commonwealth Row'. The first New Zealand High Commissioner to Australia was appointed in 1943. Initially the Commission was located in various locations in Canberra but in 1973 the Chancery on Commonwealth Avenue was opened by the then Prime Minister of New Zealand, Mr Norman Kirk. The Chancery building was designed for the New Zealand Ministry of Foreign Affairs by the Ministry of Works.

Two striking features of the building are the copper-sheathed roof and the vertical copper finished columns which provide structural support and shade. New Zealand marble and timber were used in the building. The landscaped gardens feature many New Zealand plants such as flax and cabbage trees. The trees at the front of the Chancery are a picture in spring when they are in blossom. A beautiful bronze sculpture by Tanya Ashken titled *Seabird V* is visible among the trees. Great favourites amongst Canberrans are the corrugated iron sculptures of multi-coloured cows, a work by Jeff Thomson, which graze upon the lawns at the rear of the chancery.

High Commission of New Zealand cows (2001)

Waitangi Day is New Zealand's National Day, observed each year on 6 February. The day commemorates the first signing of New Zealand's founding document, the Treaty of Waitangi in 1840. Representatives of the British Crown and over 500 Maori chiefs signed the document. The day was first officially commemorated in 1934, and it has been a public holiday since 1974. Maori cultural performances, speeches from dignitaries and a naval salute

High Commission of New Zealand (2016)

are all part of the activities at Waitangi. Celebrations happen all over New Zealand including sporting events, picnics, local food stalls, music and other entertainment.

The New Zealand flag has a royal blue background derived from the ensign of the Blue Squadron of the Royal Navy. The stars of the Southern Cross reflect the country's location in the South Pacific Ocean. The New Zealand flag was statutorily recognised in 1902 but has been in wide usage since 1869 and recognises the country's historical origins as a British colony and dominion. In 2016 New Zealanders voted to change the flag but 57% of voters opted for the current flag.

Unfortunately, due to recent developments around the world, the Chancery has had to construct security measures on its perimeter. The design is in collaboration with its Commonwealth neighbours.

High Commission of Papua New Guinea

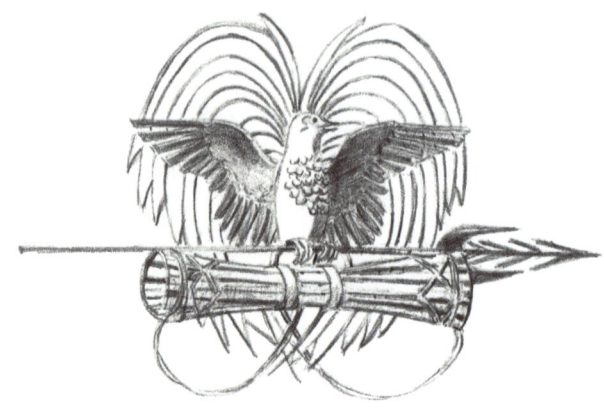

Papua New Guinea coat of arms (2003)

Papua New Guinea, Australia's nearest neighbour, occupies the eastern part of the world's second largest island as well as several off shore islands including Manus, New Britain, New Ireland and Bougainville. The western part of the island is Indonesian controlled and known as Irian Jaya.

Administered by Australia for more than seventy years, Papua New Guinea gained its independence in 1975. Linguistically it is a diverse country with more than 800 languages.

Papua New Guinea has been represented in Canberra since 1975. The chancery was officially opened in 1981 by Sir Julius Chan, the then Prime minister of the country. The Chancery of the Papua New Guinea High Commission is a striking building in the form of a *Haus Tamberan* (Spirit House) from the Sepik River region, the home of Papua New Guinea's founding prime minister, Grand Chief Sir Michael Somare. Spirit Houses are meeting places for tribal elders and storehouses for sacred objects. Roofed in timber shingles, it features 14-metre-tall gables, with stylised tribal masks painted in red, ochre, black and white at each end. Unlike the spirit houses in Papua New Guinea which are constructed of bamboo and palm fronds, modern building materials were used and its open sides enclosed for Canberra's colder climate.

Most of the timber used in the building was imported from Papua New Guinea.

High Commission of Papua New Guinea (2003)

The High Commission has a great collection of artefacts representing the many regions of the country. Included are shields, spears, masks, axes and wooden bowls.

Four totem poles stand in the grounds of the Commission. These were carved by students from the National Art School in Port Moresby. One totem pole usually stands outside the house of the village chief. The presence of four totem poles points to the symbolic importance accorded to the High Commission.

16 September is celebrated as the National Day commemorating the country's independence. Celebrations include traditional dances, art shows and sport carnivals.

The Papua New Guinea flag was officially adopted on 24 June 1971. It consists of two diagonal sections, black and red. Five-pointed white stars representing the Southern Cross are in the black section while in the red section there is a yellow bird of paradise. The Coat of Arms, featuring a bird of paradise standing above a kundu drum and a ceremonial spear, is displayed at the chancery entrance.

Philippines

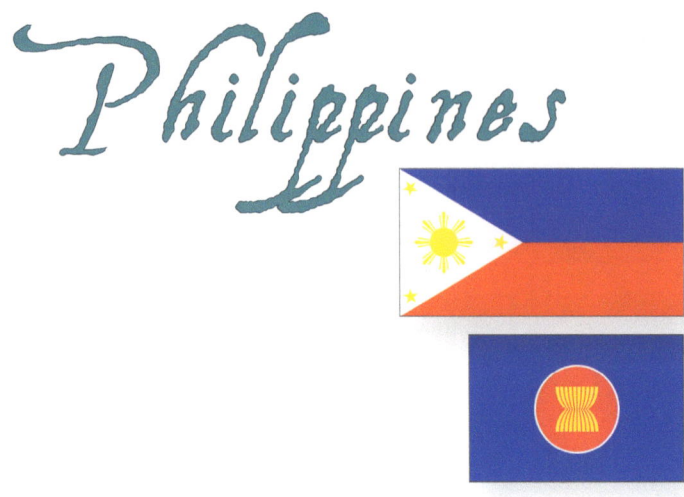

The Republic of the Philippines is an archipelago set in the western Pacific Ocean. Australia and the Philippines established diplomatic relations in 1946 and, three years later, a Philippines Legation was opened in Sydney. The Chancery and Ambassador's Residence in Canberra were built in 1962-63 and occupied in December 1963.

The Chancery design is modern contemporary, with vertical and horizontal beams, wide windows and galvanized iron roofing. Moir and Slater of Canberra were the architects following a plan by Federico Ilustre of the Philippines.

The Republic Day, also known as Independence Day, is celebrated on 12 June. It marks the date in 1898 when General Emilio Aguinaldo proclaimed independence in Kawit, in the province of Cavite from more than three centuries of Spanish rule.

Every year, the Philippine President leads the commemoration of Philippine Independence in various historical places in the Philippines. The President also hosts a *vin d'honneur* to celebrate Independence Day with the diplomatic corps. Flag raising ceremonies are held in the morning on the site of the original Independence Proclamation in 1898. In the afternoon a civilian-military parade is held in Manila, the Capital. Commemoration ceremonies take place in all major cities throughout the country. In Canberra, there is a flag-raising ceremony at the grounds of the Philippine Embassy with a diplomatic reception held subsequently to commemorate the event.

The symbols in the Philippine flag are deeply rooted in the history of the Philippine revolution. The flag is made up of three fields; a blue band at the top, a red band at the bottom, and a white equilateral triangle on the hoist side. At the centre of the triangle is a yellow sun with eight rays and at each corner of the triangle is a small yellow five-pointed star. The eight rays of the sun represent the eight provinces which rose against the Spanish rule. The three stars represent the archipelago's three principal islands - Luzon, Mindanao and Panay – where the revolution started.

The flag of the Association of Southeast Asian Nations (ASEAN) also flies in the Embassy

Philippines Embassy entrance (2003)

grounds. The Philippines became a foundation member of the ASEAN when it was established in 1967.

In January 2001, the former Philippines Ambassador, Delia Domingo Albert became the first woman to assume the role of Dean of the Diplomatic Corps in Australia.

In a Presidential Proclamation in 2016, President Benigno S. Aquino III designated 22 May as the Philippines-Australia Friendship Day.

Poland

Wall hanging view of Warsaw made with Australian wool (2001)

The Republic of Poland is a nation in east central Europe. Situated on the northern side by the Baltic Sea, neighbouring countries include Germany, the Czech Republic, Slovakia, Ukraine, Belarus, and the Russian province of Kaliningrad.

The Chancery and Ambassador's residence were built in the late seventies after Australia established diplomatic relations with Poland in 1972. Designed in Australia, the solid two-storey, white brick and concrete building has an imposing position, situated on the side of a hill. A distinctive feature is the projecting first floor which gives sun protection to the ground floor offices. The residence at the rear of the chancery is built in the same style.

Poland's National Day, November 11, marks the anniversary of the country's independence in 1918, after 123 years of partitions by Austria-Hungary, Germany and Russia. In 1939, when Poland became a communist regime the holiday was abolished. However, in 1989 when Poland became the first of the eastern European countries to overthrow communist rule, the holiday was reinstated. The day is celebrated with parades, concerts, fireworks, flag displays, and a special 10 kilometre Independence Run in the capital city, Warsaw. In Canberra the Embassy would hold a reception.

Poland's flag, a horizontal bicolour of white and red, was officially adopted in August 1919. The colours are derived from the Polish Coat of Arms, a white crowned eagle with a golden beak and talons on a red shield. The red and white colours have been associated with Poland since the 1200s while the white eagle has been used since the 1300s. The colours were officially adopted as the colours of the Polish State by the Sejm (parliament) of the Kingdom of Poland in 1831. The first recorded use

Embassy of Poland (2001)

of the Polish Coat of Arms dates from the 13th century and has gone through many changes since that time.

A second flag flying next to the national flag is that of the European Union which Poland joined in May 2004.

Poland's association with Australia dates as early as 1696 when a number of Polish crew members were on board the Dutch naval expedition exploring the western Australian coast. A Polish explorer, Paul Edmund Strzelecki, arrived in Sydney in 1839. He explored the Snowy Mountains in 1840, published the first map of Gippsland, and climbed and named Australia's highest peak, Mount Kosciuszko, after the great Polish freedom fighter and American Revolutionary War hero, Tadeusz Kosciuszko. There are about 20 geographical features in Australia bearing his name, including the Strzelecki Ranges. During the gold rushes of the 1850s many Poles came and settled in Victoria.

Saudi Arabia

The Kingdom of Saudi Arabia is a Middle Eastern country covering most of the Arabian Peninsula. It is bordered on the west by the Red Sea and on the east by the Arabian Gulf. Neighbouring countries are Jordan, Iraq, Kuwait, Qatar, Yemen, the United Arab Emirates, Oman, and Bahrain. Saudi Arabia is the birth-place of Islam.

Diplomatic relations with Australia were established in 1981 and an Embassy office was established in O'Malley. The current Royal Embassy of Saudi Arabia, both Chancery and Ambassador's residence, dates from June 1998. The extensive two-storey buildings of the Embassy are typical of the traditional architecture of the Saudi homeland. Designed by the Australian architect Philip Cox, the attractive buildings feature white walls, small windows, and narrow red roofs. All these features are necessary in Saudi Arabia due to their harsh climate.

23 September marks the National Day for Saudi Arabia, commemorating the foundation of the modern Kingdom. Previously the Arabian Peninsula had been divided into four regions, but in 1932 Saudi Arabia was united into one sovereign state by King Abdul Aziz Al-Saud, (known as the Lion of Najd). The day is a national holiday and all across the country various traditional ceremonies are held. These include folklore and dance performances, recreational and sporting activities, flag displays and parades, as well as fireworks displays at night. Saudis are particularly proud of their country's progress since unification. The Embassy in Canberra has its own celebrations.

The flag of Saudi Arabia was officially adopted in 1973. It is a green flag featuring a white Arabic inscription and a sword. The inscription on the flag, written in the Thuluth script is the shahada or Islamic declaration of faith (translated as 'There is no god but God; and Muhammad is the messenger of God'). The green of the flag represents Islam and the sword stands for the House of Saud, the founding dynasty of the country, and symbolizes the military strength and prowess of Saudi Arabia.

The official emblem of Saudi Arabia features a date palm, representing vitality and growth and two crossed swords symbolizing justice and strength.

Embassy of Saudi Arabia (2007)

High Commission of Singapore

Singapore comprises the main island of Singapore and 63 offshore islands, with Malaysia, Brunei and Indonesia as neighbours.

The first Singapore High Commissioner to Australia was appointed in 1965. The present Chancery of the High Commission of the Republic of Singapore was opened in 1985. The residence of the High Commissioner is in the suburb of Red Hill.

The very modern chancery was designed by the Canberra architects Darryl Jackson, Alastair Swayn and Peter Rees. The building won an architectural award in 1985, in the form of a Canberra Medallion, from the Royal Australian Institute of Architects, ACT Branch. A plaque at the front entrance recognises the award.

Singapore celebrates its National Day on the 9th of August. The day commemorates Singapore's Independence from Malaysia in 1965. Two years earlier Singapore, Malaya, Sarawak and Sabah formed a union which resulted in the Federation of Malaysia. Singapore withdrew from the Malaysian Federation due to political and ethnic differences, and became a fully independent and sovereign nation. National Day is celebrated very enthusiastically by the people of Singapore as they are very proud of the country's progress since independence. The big highlight is the National Day parade. The parade includes members of Singapore's military, police, civil defence force, various labour unions, community groups, business representatives and students. After the parade there are various shows and in the evening there is a huge fireworks display.

In 1959 a new flag was created to represent Singapore after it became a self-governing state under British rule. Upon independence from Malaysia, in 1965, it was adopted as the national flag. The flag consists of two equal horizontal sections, an upper red section and a lower white section. A white crescent moon and five stars are in the upper red section. The red colour represents universal brotherhood and the equality of man, while white shows purity and virtue. The crescent moon represents a rising young nation while the five stars depict Singapore's ideals of democracy, peace, progress, justice and equality.

High Commission of Singapore (2001)

The National Coat of Arms consists of a shield graced with a white crescent moon and five white stars against a red background just like the flag. Supporting the shield are a lion on the left and a tiger on the right. Below the shield is a banner inscribed with the Republic's motto, *Majulah Singapura* (Onward Singapore).

Singapore was a founding member of (ASEAN) when it was formed in 1967.

High Commission of South Africa

South African High Commission residence (2002)

The Republic of South Africa stretches from Cape Agulhas at the southern tip of the African continent to its borders, to the north and north-east, with Namibia, Botswana, Zimbabwe and Mozambique. It is bounded by a long coastline with the Atlantic Ocean to the west and the Indian Ocean to the east.

Australia and South Africa established diplomatic relations in 1947. The High Commissioner's residence was built in 1956/7 and the current Chancery in 1968. Both the Chancery and residence are constructed in Cape Dutch style with whitewashed walls and timber framed sash windows. The entrance to the residence, South Africa House, is particularly attractive with a charming garden, and colonial lights at the entrance gates. The architects were Moir and Slater of Canberra.

Freedom Day, 27 April, is South Africa's national day. It is a celebration of the country's first non-racial democratic elections in 1994. After three hundred years of colonialism, segregation and white minority rule a new democratic government was established led by Nelson Mandela. A public holiday, rallies are held in large stadiums, addresses are made by the country's leaders, plays and other entertainment all mark the day. In Canberra a reception is held at South Africa House.

The National Flag of the Republic of South Africa was adopted on April 27th 1994, following the democratic elections. The design and colours of the new National Flag are a synopsis of the principal elements of South Africa's flag history, from the earliest days to the present time. Although the colours have no official meaning, the black, green and yellow were the colours of Nelson Mandela's political party, the

South African High Commission (2003)

African National Congress. The red, white and blue are the colours of the former Boer republic flags. The Y shape represents the convergence of South Africa's diverse society and the desire for unity.

South Africa's Coat of Arms was launched by President Mbeki on Freedom Day, 27 April 2000. Containing many symbols of South African life, including the secretary bird, a protea, ears of wheat, tusks of the African elephant, a spear which contains images of Khoisan people, the first inhabitants of the land. The Motto on the base is written in Khoisan language and means diverse people unite.

The world famous South African surgeon, Dr Christian Barnard, who led the team that performed the first human to human heart transplant, planted a blue spruce tree in front of South Africa House, on a visit in 1968.

Spain

Spain established diplomatic relations with Australia when Mr Ramon Parellada was appointed as Consul-general in Sydney in 1967 and, in December 1968, as the first Ambassador of Spain in Canberra.

The official Embassy of Spain was opened in the early 1980s and in 1988 the original two-storey structure was extended and given its current appearance, being inaugurated on 1 July 1990 by His Royal Highness, Prince Felipe de Asturias.

The chancery is connected by walkways to a building of similar size at the rear. The ground floor has two Andalusian patios typical of southern Spain where the dry and sunny weather encourages outside gatherings. The white outside walls are typical of many southern villages and houses.

The architecture might remind the viewer of an American Spanish colonial church with its long nave in the centre connecting the symmetrical wings of the chancery. The glass enclosed balconies that cover the façade and the long glass panels of the nave add a contemporary and modern touch to this Spanish neo-colonial style.

The architects were Maria de los Angeles Hernandez Rubio of the Spanish Ministry of Foreign Affairs and Tom Kean and Carlos Miranda of Woods Bagot of Canberra.

An unusual feature of the chancery is the nine by six metre mural of an Australian model called 'Sarah' created by street artist Rone. The Melbourne based artist, who specialises in larger than life images of hauntingly beautiful faces, was invited by the embassy to decorate a street facing wall on their building after winning their urban art prize in 2015.

An exhibition of Spanish exploration at the National Museum of Australia in 2007 contributed to the historic connections between Spain and Australia. Entitled 'Spanish Expeditions to the South Pacific from the 16th to the 18th centuries', the exhibition marked the 400th anniversary of the voyages of Luis Vaez de Torres and Pedro Fernandez de Quiros. Almost 200 years before Captain Cook charted the east coast, Torres sailed between Australia and New Guinea through the strait which still bears his name.

Canberra's Embassies

Entrance to the Embassy of Spain (2016)

Spain was discovering and establishing its presence in the Pacific at this time.

The discovery and exploration of new continents and oceans have been an essential part of the history of Spain and even its national day, also known as Hispanic day, is celebrated on the 12 October, which commemorates the arrival of Columbus in the Americas in 1492.

Two flags fly outside the Embassy, the current national flag, officially adopted in December 1981 and the flag of the EU which Spain joined in 1986 when it was known as the EEC. The national flag consists of three horizontal bands, two reds, top and bottom and a yellow double width band in the centre which includes the Spanish coat of arms.

Sweden

Sweden has had a long association with Australia. Dr. Daniel Carl Solander, a Swedish naturalist, accompanied Captain Cook on his first voyage between 1768 and 1770. Today he is remembered with a street named after him—Solander Place, in the embassy suburb of Yarralumla.

The Swedish Embassy, one of the first overseas missions to be established in Canberra, was built between 1947 and 1951. The length of building time was due to post war shortages of materials and labour.

The architects were Peddle, Thorp and Walker of Sydney who developed the design from sketch plans by a Swedish architect, Mr E G H Lundquist. The building, which was Scandinavian in style but adapted to suit Australian climatic conditions, received the 1952 Sir John Sulman Award for outstanding architecture. It was the first building in Canberra to receive this honour and the first by a foreign country. The building encompasses the ambassador's residence, the chancery and embassy staff accommodation. The coats of arms over the chancery and ambassador's entrances were carved in Sweden from Gotland sandstone.

Unlike many other embassies in Canberra the elegant Swedish building cannot be seen from the street. It is set well back on a huge block, the garden featuring mature eucalyptus and conifers.

For many years Sweden had no official national day. From June 6th 1916 'Flag Day' began to be celebrated. This date commemorates the day in 1523 when Gustav Vasa, who delivered the country from the previously enforced union with Denmark, was elected King of Sweden. In addition, one of Sweden's constitutions was signed on 6th June 1809. It became the custom that on June 6th the King would present flags to representatives of various corporations at a festive ceremony, subsequently known as Flag Day. It was not until 1983 that June 6th became the official national day. Today it is a working day, not a

Entrance to the Embassy of Sweden (2002)

holiday, as in other countries. flag presentations and ceremonial speeches are usually held in the evening. Sweden joined the EU in 1995 and the EU flag flies with the national flag in the embassy grounds. The Swedish flag features a yellow cross on a blue background, and was made into law on June 22nd 1906.

A special event on the Swedish calendar is Walpurgis Night on the 30th April. Celebrated on the eve of the feast of St. Walpurga, it marks the end of winter and the beginning of spring and is an occasion for choral singing and bonfires. The Swedish Embassy follows the tradition even though the seasons are reversed.

Switzerland

Switzerland is located in western and central Europe and bordered by Germany, France, Italy, Austria and Liechtenstein. It was transformed from a loose federation of different cantons into the present confederation with a central government in 1848. The Swiss national flag has been officially in use ever since. It is a red square with a white cross on the centre that does not extend to the borders of the flag.

Since 1891, the first of August has been celebrated as Swiss National Day. The date was chosen because the Federal Charter (Bundesbrief) of 1291 was dated 'at the beginning of the month of August'. Considered one of the country's most important founding documents, it unified three cantons in the geographical heart of modern day Switzerland.

Switzerland has had a long association with Australia. The first Swiss to set foot on Australian soil is believed to be the artist Johann Waber (John Webber) who accompanied Captain Cook as an illustrator on his third voyage. The first major arrival of Swiss emigrants began in the 1830s when a number of wine growers emigrated from Switzerland and helped to make Victoria an important wine-growing area. Many Swiss people also arrived during the gold rushes in the mid-nineteenth century.

Switzerland opened a consulate in Sydney in 1855 and in Melbourne in 1856. Formal diplomatic relations were initiated in 1961 when Switzerland opened an Embassy in Canberra. The current Embassy building was established in 1975. It is a long, modern two-storey building, set on high ground, with a bushland setting and a commanding view. The design was chosen from a competition held in 1970 in which Australian and Swiss architects were invited to participate. Hermann Baur and his son Hans Peter of Basel, Switzerland, were awarded the project. The Embassy building was honoured with a design award by the Royal Australian Institute of Architects in 2004. The award, known as the 25-year award for sustained architectural excellence, recognises buildings that exhibit fine design qualities and continue to enhance the urban environment.

Canberra's Embassies

Embassy of Switzerland (2003)

Thailand

The Kingdom of Thailand is located in south-east Asia and shares borders with Myanmar, Laos, Cambodia, and Malaysia. Unlike many other Asian nations, Thailand was never colonised by Europeans.

In 1952 Thailand sent a delegation to Australia to negotiate diplomatic representation and the following year a legation was established in Canberra. In1956 the status of the legation was raised to an embassy. The ambassador's residence was built in 1970-1971 in typical Thai style with elevated roof design, upswept roof corners and gold and white roof tiles. The Australian architect was Mr T N Olgay of Stephenson and Turner. A Thai architect, Mr Paiboon Arthayukti, was responsible for the roof design. The Crown Prince of Thailand, His Royal Highness Prince Vajiralongkorn, officiated at the opening of the residence on 18 September 1971. The chancery was built in the same style in 1975. The new chancery and the Thai Pavilion (*Sala Thai*) were built during 1996-1998 and officially opened on 14th July 1998.

The Thai National Day is celebrated on 28 July, the birthday of their King Maha Vajiralong Korn, who ascended to the throne on the death of his highly respected father, King Bhumibol Adulyadej in October 2016. The day is celebrated with candle-lit ceremonies and fireworks across the country.

Thailand's flag was officially adopted on 28 September, 1917. The flag consists of five horizontal stripes. The top and bottom are equal sized red stripes representing the Nation and Thai people. In the middle of the flag the large blue stripe is lined by equal-sized white stripes. Blue is Thailand's national colour and also represents the Thai monarchy. White stands for purity and religion. While Thais are predominately Buddhists, all religions are tolerated and protected under the Constitution.

There is a second flag flying in front of the embassy. It is the flag of ASEAN of which Thailand was a founding member in 1967.

Thai Embassy praying figure statue (2003)

Embassy of Thailand (2003)

Thailand has no coat of arms but has a national symbol known as the *Phra Khrut Pha*. The symbol, which was adopted in 1911, is a *Garuda*, a mythical half-man half-bird being in Hindu mythology. The mythical bird has been used as the Royal symbol and later as the national seal and the seal of the government of Thailand.

Every year the Royal Thai Embassy holds a food and cultural festival in September. Thai products and handicrafts are on show, dancing and martial arts are displayed and wonderful food is on hand supplied by many of Canberra's great Thai restaurants. It is a very popular event.

Turkey

The Republic of Turkey lies predominately in Asia and partly in Europe. The country has significant sea borders, Black Sea to the north, Aegean to the west, and Mediterranean to the south. Land neighbours include Greece, Bulgaria, Russia, Ukraine, Romania, Georgia, Armenia, Azerbaijan, Iran, Syria, and Iraq.

Turkey and Australia established diplomatic relations in 1967, when the first Turkish Ambassador to Australia was appointed. Originally the embassy was in Red Hill.

The existing Chancery was opened in 2006, and following the tradition of using architecture from the country of origin, it has features of Turkish civil architecture combined with Australian architecture, creating a contemporary building set within a unique surrounding landscape. It features Turkish artistic, cultural and aesthetic heritage. Turkish roofing style, tiles placed on facade, tulip shaped balcony fences, and elongated window frames are the main distinctive features. Blue Turkish tiles are subtly embedded in the sandstone columns around the Chancery. The garden design is traditional Ottoman style and 20,000 tulip bulbs have been planted. Tulips, the Turkish national flower, are native to Asia Minor and were smuggled to Holland in the 16th century. The garden features traditional Turkish flora, pine trees, lemon trees and rosemaries and Australian indigenous plants and trees. Red and white roses have been planted facing State Circle.

Embassy of Turkey flag (2016)

The Chancery building was designed by Mr Wal Kostyrko, and officially inaugurated by H E Mr Cemil Cicek, then Minister of Justice of the Republic of Turkey, and Alexander Downer, Minister for Foreign Affairs of Australia, on 25 August 2006.

The National Day of Turkey, (Republic Day), is celebrated on October 29 each year. It marks the creation of the Turkish Republic in 1923 and is the most important day of modern Turkey. After the War of Independence, the Turkish Parliament proclaimed the new Turkey as a Republic, and Mustafa Kemal

Embassy of Turkey (2016)

Ataturk, the founder of the Republic and leader of the independence war, became the first President of Turkey. The day is celebrated with parades, official ceremonies, theatre performances, music and traditional Turkish dances. In Canberra a reception is held.

The Turkish flag features a white crescent and a white star on a red background. Although the crescent and star are traditional symbols of the Islamic religion, the crescent moon and star in the Turkish flag pre-date Islam and are not meant to represent the religion. The red colour on the flag represents the blood of those who sacrificed their lives during the course of Turkish history. The Turkish flag is called *Ay Yildz* meaning moon star.

High Commission of United Kingdom

United Kingdon High Commssion front entrance (2016)

The United Kingdom of Great Britain and Northern Ireland, more commonly known as either the United Kingdom or Britain, consists of four countries: England, Scotland, Wales and Northern Ireland.

The Union Jack is the national flag of the United Kingdom and was officially adopted in 1801.

Westminster House front (2002)

The Union Jack combines aspects of the older national flags: the red cross of St George of the Kingdom of England, the white saltire of St Andrew for Scotland, and the red saltire of St Patrick to represent Ireland. Wales is indirectly represented through the Kingdom of England which included Wales.

The four countries in The United Kingdom each have an individual National Day all honouring a patron saint. England commemorates St George's Day on the 23rd April, Scotland honours St Andrew's Day on the 30th of November, Wales marks St David's Day on 1st March and Northern Ireland celebrates St Patrick's Day on 17th March.

The United Kingdom has a prominent voice on the world stage as permanent members of the UN Security Council, of the North Atlantic Treaty Organisation (NATO), of the G7, the G20 and the Commonwealth.

Garden at the rear of Westminster House (2002)

Prior to 1936, the Governor-General of Australia was the official representative of the British Government, as well as of the monarch. The first British High Commissioner, Sir Geoffrey Whiskard, was appointed in 1936. In 1952 the British High Commission Chancery building in Yarralumla, and Westminster House, the official residence of the High Commissioner, were built, both designed by architects E.A. and T.M. Scott of Sydney.

Major refurbishments, designed by Mitchell, Giurgola and Thorp, the architects who designed Parliament House, were made to the Chancery from 1995 until 1997. The renovated building was opened by the the then Australian Prime minister, John Howard, and the then High Commissioner, Sir John Carrick on 5 February 1997.

Originally the main entrance was from Commonwealth Avenue but today the public entrance is from Forster Crescent, facing the Chinese Embassy. A tribute sculpture by Stephen Cox, a well-known English artist, is in the front garden and was the site of many floral tributes to mark the death of Princess Diana in 1997.

Westminster House is situated on a very large block surrounded by a magnificent garden and is used for most of the High Commissions social functions. Of interest is the impressive sculpture, Arch Stones, by the English sculptor, John Maine, on the lawns of Westminster House.

United States of America

The first recorded contact of the United States with Australia came in 1792 when the United States ship *Philadelphia* sailed into Sydney. Later trading ships and whaling vessels arrived. In 1833 American merchants opened trading branches and the first Consul was appointed in Sydney in 1836.

Official diplomatic relations were not established until January 1940 when Ministers were exchanged. Previously all contacts were made through the United Kingdom Government. In September 1946 the first American Ambassador to Australia arrived.

The property occupied by the United States Embassy is one of the largest in the capital, the site being 9.6 acres. It is interesting to note that the lease for the land was signed on the same day (Australian time) that the Japanese struck Pearl Harbour, December 8 1941. The American Embassy was the first purpose built embassy established in Canberra. Built in Georgian style, the construction was inspired by the buildings in Williamsburg, the original capital of Colonial Virginia, which were designed by Christopher Wren. Williamsburg was a centre of liberty and freedom in colonial times. The whole compound comprises the Chancery, Ambassador's residence and various other administrative buildings. The Canberra brickworks supplied the façade bricks to match samples sent from Williamsburg, and they were made to the exact design, colour, texture and size. Unfortunately, when later extensions were undertaken, the bricks had to be sent from Virginia as the original Canberra kiln had ceased operations. Tight security surrounds the compound.

The architects for the embassy included several from the Foreign Buildings Office of the State Department in Washington DC, as well as the local supervising architect, Malcolm Moir, of Moir and Sutherland. The unique architecture of the embassy design initiated a trend for many other countries to build their embassies in a style reflecting their homelands' architecture. These embassies give rise to the title of this book, *International Treasures*.

Residence United States of America (2002)

Among the many dignitaries

Embassy of the United States of America (2002)

who have planted trees in the embassy garden are Presidents Lyndon Johnson, Jimmy Carter, Gerald Ford, George H. W. Bush, George W Bush and Barack Obama.

Independence Day is annually celebrated on 4 July. It is the United States National Day, commemorating the signing of the Declaration of Independence from Great Britain in 1776. A great family day in America, it is celebrated across the country as well as in United States diplomatic missions around the world.

The American flag, known as the Stars and Stripes (or colloquially as 'Old Glory') was officially adopted in 1777 but has gone through several revisions since that time. Today the flag comprises 13 horizontal stripes, seven red and six white. In the upper left corner there are fifty white five pointed stars on a blue background. The stripes represent the original thirteen colonies and the fifty white five-pointed stars, the 50 States of the Union.

Foreign Embassies in Australia

(Correct as at 16 November 2017)

Country	Address
Embassy of the Islamic Republic of Afghanistan	4 Beale Crescent, Deakin ACT 2600
Embassy of the People's Democratic Republic of Algeria	29 Cobbadah Street, O'Malley ACT 2606
Embassy of the Argentine Republic	John McEwen House, 7 National Circuit, Barton ACT 2600
Embassy of Austria	12 Talbot Street, Forrest ACT 2603
Embassy of the Republic of Azerbaijan	5 Mialli Place, O'Malley ACT 2606
High Commission for the People's Republic of Bangladesh	57 Culgoa Circuit, O'Malley ACT 2606
Embassy of the Republic of Belarus	31 Guilfoyle Street, Yarralumla ACT 2600
Royal Belgium Embassy	19 Arkana Street, Yarralumla ACT 2600
Embassy of Bosnia & Herzegovina	5 Beale Crescent, Deakin ACT 2600
High Commission of the Republic of Botswana	130 Denison Street, Deakin ACT 2600
Embassy of the Federative Republic of Brazil	19 Forster Crescent, Yarralumla ACT 2600
High Commission of Brunei Darussalam	10 Beale Crescent, Deakin ACT 2600
Embassy of Bulgaria	29 Pindari Crescent, O'Malley ACT 2606
Royal Embassy of Cambodia	5 Canterbury Crescent, Deakin ACT 2600
Embassy of the Republic of Costa Rica	15 London Circuit, Suite 903, Canberra ACT 2601
Embassy of the Republic of Côte d'Ivoire	6 Berbet Street, O'Malley ACT 2606
High Commission of Canada	Commonwealth Avenue, Canberra ACT 2600
Embassy of the Republic of Chile	10 Culgoa Circuit, O'Malley ACT 2606
Embassy of the People's Republic of China	15 Coronation Drive, Yarralumla ACT 2600
Embassy of the Republic of Colombia	Level 2, 40 Macquarie Street, Barton ACT 2600
Embassy of the Republic of Croatia	14 Jindalee Crescent, O'Malley ACT 2606
Embassy of the Republic of Cuba	17 Terrigal Crescent, O'Malley ACT 2606
High Commission of the Republic of Cyprus	30 Beale Crescent, Deakin ACT 2600

Embassy of the Czech Republic	8 Culgoa Circuit, O'Malley ACT 2606
Royal Danish Embassy	15 Hunter Street, Yarralumla ACT 2600
Embassy of the Republic of Ecuador	6 Pindari Crescent, O'Malley ACT 2606
Embassy of the Arab Republic of Egypt	1 Darwin Avenue, Yarralumla ACT 2600
Embassy of the Republic of El Salvador	3/110 Giles Street, Kingston ACT 2604
Embassy of the Republic of Estonia	12 Darwin Avenue, Yarralumla ACT 2600
Embassy of the Federal Democratic Republic of Ethiopia	3 Sirius Place, Red Hill ACT 2603
Delegation of the European Union	18 Arkana Street, Yarralumla ACT 2600
High Commission of the Republic of Fiji	19 Beale Crescent, Deakin ACT 2600
Embassy of Finland	12 Darwin Avenue, Yarralumla ACT 2600
Embassy of France	6 Perth Avenue, Yarralumla ACT 2600
Embassy of Georgia	28 Kareelah Vista, O'Malley ACT 2606
Embassy of the Federal Republic of Germany	119 Empire Circuit, Yarralumla ACT 2600
High Commission of the Republic of Ghana	52 Culgoa Circuit, O'Malley ACT 2606
Embassy of Greece	9 Turrana Street, Yarralumla ACT 2600
Embassy of the Republic of Guatemala	Unit 9, 11 National Circuit, Barton ACT 2600
Apostolic Nunciature Holy See	2 Vancouver Street, Red Hill ACT 2603
Embassy of Hungary	17 Beale Crescent, Deakin ACT 2600
High Commission of India	3-5 Moonah Place, Yarralumla ACT 2600
Embassy of the Republic of Indonesia	8 Darwin Avenue, Yarralumla ACT 2600
Embassy of the Islamic Republic of Iran	25 Culgoa Circuit, O'Malley ACT 2606
Embassy of the Republic of Iraq	48 Culgoa Circuit, O'Malley ACT 2606
Embassy of Ireland	20 Arkana Street, Yarralumla ACT 2600
Embassy of Israel	6 Turrana Street, Yarralumla ACT 2600
Embassy of Italy	12 Grey Street, Deakin ACT 2600
Embassy of Japan	112 Empire Circuit, Yarralumla ACT 2600
Embassy of the Hashemite Kingdom of Jordan	17 Cobbadah Street, O'Malley ACT 2606
High Commission of the Republic of Kenya	43 Culgoa Circuit, O'Malley ACT 2606
Embassy of the Republic of Korea	113 Empire Circuit, Yarralumla ACT 2600

Embassy of the Republic of Kosovo	25 Numeralla Street, O'Malley ACT 2606
Embassy of the State of Kuwait	5 Callemonda Rise, O'Malley ACT 2606
Embassy of the Lao People's Democratic Republic	1 Dalman Crescent, O'Malley ACT 2606
Embassy of Lebanon	27 Endeavour Street, Red Hill ACT 2603
Embassy of Libya	50 Culgoa Circuit, O'Malley ACT 2606
Embassy of the former Yugoslav Republic of Macedonia	25 Cobbadah Street, O'Malley ACT 2606
High Commission of Malaysia	7 Perth Avenue, Yarralumla ACT 2600
High Commission of Malta	38 Culgoa Circuit, O'Malley ACT 2606
High Commission of the Republic of Mauritius	2 Beale Crescent, Deakin ACT 2600
Embassy of Mexico	14 Perth Avenue, Yarralumla ACT 2600
Embassy of Mongolia	23 Culgoa Circuit, O'Malley ACT 2606
Embassy of the Kingdom of Morocco	9 Terrigal Crescent, O'Malley ACT 2606
Embassy of the Republic of the Union of Myanmar	22 Arkana Street, Yarralumla ACT 2600
Embassy of Nepal	22 Kareelah Vista, O'Malley ACT 2606
Embassy of the Kingdom of the Netherlands	120 Empire Circuit, Yarralumla ACT 2600
New Zealand High Commission	140 Commonwealth Avenue, Canberra ACT 2600
High Commission of the Federal Republic of Nigeria	26 Guilfoyle Street, Yarralumla ACT 2600
Royal Norwegian Embassy	17 Hunter Street, Yarralumla ACT 2600
High Commission of Pakistan	4 Perth Avenue, Yarralumla ACT 2600
High Commission of Papua New Guinea	39-41 Forster Crescent, Yarralumla ACT 2600
Embassy of Paraguay	39 Empire Circuit, Forrest ACT 2603
Embassy of the Republic of Peru	40 Brisbane Avenue, Barton ACT 2600
Embassy of the Philippines	1 Moonah Place, Yarralumla ACT 2600
Embassy of the Republic of Poland	7 Turrana Street, Yarralumla ACT 2600
Embassy of Portugal	Stephen House, 32 Thesiger Court, Deakin ACT 2600
Embassy of the State of Qatar	10 Akame Circuit, O'Malley ACT 2606
Embassy of Romania	4 Dalman Crescent, O'Malley ACT 2606
Embassy of the Russian Federation	78 Canberra Avenue, Griffith ACT 2603
High Commission of Samoa	3 Darwin Avenue, Yarralumla ACT 2600

Royal Embassy of Saudi Arabia	38 Guilfoyle Street, Yarralumla ACT 2600
Embassy of the Republic of Serbia	4 Bulwarra Close, O'Malley ACT 2606
High Commission of the Republic of Singapore	17 Forster Crescent, Yarralumla ACT 2600
Embassy of the Slovak Republic	47 Culgoa Circuit, O'Malley ACT 2606
Embassy of the Republic of Slovenia	26 Akame Circuit, O'Malley ACT 2606
Solomon Islands High Commission	1 Beale Crescent, Deakin ACT 2060
South African High Commission	Cnr State Circle and Rhodes Place, Yarralumla ACT 2600
Embassy of Spain	15 Arkana Street, Yarralumla ACT 2600
High Commission of the Democratic Socialist Republic of Sri Lanka	61 Hampton Circuit, Yarralumla ACT 2600
Embassy of the Republic of The Sudan	23 Numeralla Street, O'Malley ACT 2606
Embassy of Sweden	5 Turrana Street, Yarralumla ACT 2600
Embassy of Switzerland	7 Melbourne Avenue, Forrest ACT 2603
Royal Thai Embassy	111 Empire Circuit, Yarralumla ACT 2600
Embassy of the Democratic Republic of Timor-Leste	7 Beale Crescent, Deakin ACT 2600
High Commission of the Kingdom of Tonga	7 Newdegate Street, Deakin ACT 2600
Embassy of the Republic of Tunisia	3 Callemonda Rise, O'Malley ACT 2606
Embassy of the Republic of Turkey	6 Moonah Place, Yarralumla ACT 2600
High Commission of the Republic of Uganda	11 Ngunnawal Drive, O'Malley ACT 2605
Embassy of Ukraine	St George Centre, 60 Marcus Clarke Street, Canberra ACT 2601
Embassy of the United Arab Emirates	12 Bulwarra Close, O'Malley ACT 2606
Embassy of the United States of America	Moonah Place, Yarralumla ACT 2600
United Kingdom, British High Commission	Commonwealth Avenue, Yarralumla ACT 2600
Embassy of Uruguay	Suite 2, Level 4, 24 Brisbane Avenue, Barton ACT 2600
High Commission of the Republic of Vanuatu	16 Thesiger Court, Deakin ACT 2600
Embassy of the Bolivarian Republic of Venezuela	12 Keyar Street, O'Malley ACT 2606
Embassy of the Socialist Republic of Vietnam	6 Timbarra Crescent, O'Malley ACT 2606
High Commission of the Republic of Zambia	10 National Circuit, Barton ACT 26006
Embassy of the Republic of Zimbabwe	26 Numeralla Street, O'Malley ACT 2606